Owls in the Garden

Story by Andrew Kelly
Illustrations by Meredith Thomas

Katie and her two best friends, Tring and Grace, put their sleeping bags inside Katie's new tent. "Imagine!" said Tring. "We're going to sleep outside for a whole night on our own. It'll be the best thing we've done all year."

"I can hardly wait for it to get dark," said Katie.

The back door banged.
Katie's big brother Martin,
and his dog Rover, came out.
"You girls won't last five minutes
in that tent," said Martin.
"You'll be running inside crying,
'Mommy, Mommy! Something scared me.'"

"I'm not scared of anything,"
Katie told them all at dinner that night.

"I'm not even afraid of the dark,"
said Grace.

"Neither am I," said Tring.

But none of them sounded very sure.

Martin laughed loudly.
"Do you know about the ghost owl
that swoops down at night
and grabs..."

"Stop that, Martin!" said Mom.

But Martin went on,
"...grabs little girls and eats..."

"Martin!" said Dad.
"You heard your mother. Stop it."

When it was dark,
the girls changed into their sweat suits
and went out to the tent.
Katie shone her flashlight all around.

"I've got some chocolate," said Grace.
"Let's eat it now."

The girls made the chocolate
last for as long as they could.

Tring showed the others
how to make shadow animals with their hands
in the beam of Katie's flashlight.

"That wolf's head is really scary," said Grace.

"I'm going to go inside and brush my teeth,"
said Katie.

"We'll come, too," said Tring and Grace.

The girls ran across the lawn
and went into the house.

Martin laughed when he saw them, and said,
"I knew you wouldn't last five minutes!"

"We're just brushing our teeth!" said Katie.

"And then we're going straight back," said Tring.

Katie's mom walked back to the tent with the girls.
"It's okay, Mom," said Katie.
"We're not scared."

"Good night, then," said Mom.
She went back inside,
and the three of them were alone.

At first it seemed quiet outside, but soon they began to hear little noises.
The bushes rustled,
and insects buzzed around the light over the back door.

What was that? Tring sat up.
Something was sniffing
around the tent.
The side of the tent bulged.

"What is it?" whispered Grace.

"Rover, come here. Come inside."
The girls heard Katie's dad call
from the back door.
"Why did Martin let you out again?"

"It was only Rover," said Katie to the others.
"I should have guessed."

The girls were nearly asleep
when they heard another noise.
Whoo, whoo, whoo.

The sound came again.
Whoo, whoo, whoooooo.

"Do you think that's the ghost owl
Martin was talking about?"
whispered Grace.

"Are you scared?" asked Tring.
"Should we go inside?"

Whoo, whoo, whoooo!
Now the noise was closer and louder.
It seemed to come from the bushes nearby.
Katie grabbed the flashlight,
and Grace began to pull at the zipper
on the tent.

"Let's make a run for it," she said.

But then they heard another call.
It sounded different this time:
Tu-whit, tu-whoo. Tu-whit, tu-whoo.

And this time it came from the trees.

Suddenly, something burst out
of the bushes behind the tent.

The girls clutched each other.
Then they saw **Martin**
running across the lawn toward the house.

"Mom, Mom! The ghost owl!"
He shouted as he ran. "It's in our yard."

The back door opened. "Martin!
What are you doing outside?" asked Mom.

"I saw the ghost owl," Martin gasped.
"It was trying to get me!"

"There's no such thing as a ghost owl,"
said Dad. "You must have seen a real owl.
That's nothing to be scared of.
Owls don't hurt people."

"And it won't be back after all the noise
that you've been making," said Mom.

"Martin won't be back either,"
Dad told the girls.
"Now you'll be able to go to sleep."

The girls looked at each other.
Tring started to giggle,
"Imagine! Martin was frightened of an owl!"

And they all climbed back
into their sleeping bags
and laughed and laughed.